ADAPTATIONS

ADAPTATIONS

Challenges Ahead
Facing Democracy
Competitive Capitalism

CHRIS NELSON

To order additional copies of this book, contact:
Xlibris
1-888-795-4274
www.Xlibris.com
Orders@Xlibris.com
796644

CONTENTS

We begin our email by asking ourselves: What is the purpose of democratic well-run government? Answer according to poets/thinkers/philosophers: to serve the public in their own best interests (rulers must be wise/be able to make wise decisions/schooled in democratic political/economic wisdom) Webster's Dictionary of the American Language defines democracy as: Equality of Rights/Opportunity/and Treatment. The democratic ideal is equality of rights (enshrined in the constitution/equality of opportunity (ideally by making sure all have an equal chance at a decent education/livelihood/and equality of treatment (under the law everyone being guaranteed the same right as his neighbour to fair and impartial treatment). People remember the opening words spoken by Thomas Jefferson in the Declaration of Independence: (something like this): All Men Are Created Equal. What was the true intent of this statement/how should this statement best be interpreted.

Did he mean that all men were created with the same intellectual/emotional/ and physical endowments/characteristics? On the surface of it, this statement seems to be contradicted by the evidence: people come in all sorts of different shapes and sizes and colours for starters; that covers their outward appearance aspect. What about the intellectual aspect? Well we all know that some people do better at their IQ tests/SAT tests than others, that much is obvious. We also know that people come with all sorts of different artistic, literary, and musical talents, the Bible refers to these creative talents as "gifts", meaning gifts from...G. Today when Creation Idea is believed in by some/Evolution idea is believed by others/combination of both is believed by still others... it is not the easiest thing to decide wherefrom intellectual, emotional, and physical traits originate...in fact, the Canadian World Almanac and Book of

Facts (1987), says that the timing and origin of man, or homo sapiens, to use the scientific word, is "shrouded in mystery"...might have as well added, and so far as we know...always will be. What are the practical implications of this contention that the origins of man are "shrouded in mystery". Is this an anti-religious view of/outlook upon the world? Well opinions will of course differ on controversial issues but, for what it's worth,..the famous british theologian, Malcolm Muggeridge, in his book, Conversion, defined the essence of the religious outlook on life as: "accepting the utter and unfathomable mystery of human existence". I am going from memory as I don't have my 10 page summary of "what have I learned from my reading of Malcolm Muggeridge?"

What did Malcolm Muggeridge have to say that bears on the topic under discussion: the idea that on the surface of things men do "not" seem to be created/evolved/combination of both: equal??!!! Well searching my memory/ trying to pull up the facts comes to mind the following passage: the scene is Paris 1945. Two separate and apart stories of the meaning of victory, let u decide which one was the more real? and i know i am treading on sensitive ground here..scene one: the triumphant victory parade down the main thoroughfare of Paris the elegant and stately Champs-Elysees (fields of elysium, believing this to mean fields of paradise and having seen it myself from my childhood in France I can attest to it's magnificent layout widest of avenues bordered by marvellous trees, widest of sidewalks, at every step one of the charming cafes where go the Parisians and tourists to sip a coffee read the newspaper, play chess, or simply watch the passers-by on the sidewalks. (here I can't resist an aside that a glass of coke was out of my family's reach at over $3:00 which was pretty darn steep back in those days (1960's). Well i guess the price of the coke reflected/had built into it the desirability of the location??!!! Why all this going into detail about the magnificence of this great thoroughfare traversing the length and breadth of Paris? Well, it is to underline a point i wish to make about life in general: "Just as in life so in this game of scrabble spelt, it's a combination of both u and the cards (letters) ur dealt" (for those not familiar with this great game, which happens to my favourite on account of being good with words and letters, scrabble is a sort of crossword board game, where two or more players, each with seven tiles drawn closed eyes out of a bag holding 100 plus letters of the alphabet repeated; the players try out of their seven letters on their scrabble benches to form words either alone or in combination with letters words already placed on the scrabble board; always trying to place the highest score tiles on the highest score squares on the scrabble board/player with the highest sum total of points from all his letters wins after subtracting/ deducting the value of the tiles remaining on each player's bench at the end of the game when no more tiles in bag/all played).

What is the point? Again (listen carefully pls.); "just as in life, so in this game of scrabble spelt. it's a combination of both u and the cards (letters) ur dealt"; to quote further from my first published book of poems (A Single Rose Can be My Garden), cf. the following: "a lot depends on the letters u get, how well u do, but mostly in the mind, ur scrabble I.Q." and further down: "plan as u may/plan as u will/the outcome rarely fits the bill". end of quote. Well to stop beating about the bush and get to the heart of the message trying to convey by scrabble "simile/metaphor" for life: regardless what ur religious beliefs are concerning the grand issues such as origins of earth and homo sapiens; it is an undeniable fact that none of us have any control to which parents we are born/where our parents happen to live/or how wealthy our parents happen to be; same with which colour of skin/which colour of eyes/which colour of hair; which intellectual, artistic creative talents happen to blessed with.

In this sense human beings all come into the world with differing endowments of these various characteristics. In this first sense of the word "people are not created equal". But in another sense of the word they are: they all have in common that they are members of the human race, which is to say belong to same species...homo sapiens. Another way of stating this is: this is the area where their interests overlap to a greater or lesser extent, this might be called their: COMMON HUMANITY. What do i mean that their interests overlap to a greater or lesser extent. Well, it depends on/is a question of attitude of people one to another in any given society; they can either emphasize/lay stress upon the differences which keep them apart/or they place stress/emphasis on their commonalities that bring people together. Well I guess by now u can see what all this is leading up to. Again: the dictionary definition of democracy is: "equality of rights/opportunity/and treatment of ALL people in society no matter their differences: to list only a few of the main ones again in order of importance in terms of how people are impacted/fare differently on the basis of them: my list would run as follows in order of differential impact on person's rights/opportunity/and treatment: first and foremost I would put in first place interchangeably: social class (whether rich or poor or middle); racial class (whether white or black or brown); intellectual class (whether very bright or less bright); regional class (differences in opportunities between regions and between urban and rural): differences in age (whether elder or younger); differences in health (whether they are healthy in all ways, or whether they are in some way - either intellectually/emotionally or physically - challenged.) Where do we stand on this today in our N/A society? Well, if we're honest about it: we've come a long way since independence in 1776/confederation in 1867/but we still have some considerable distance to go before the ideal of equality of rights/treatment/and opportunity are observed not just on paper but in reality. What say u? Is that the real purpose of democratically well run government: not just to preach but to put into practice this marvellously simple sounding, yet very hard of achievement TRIPARTITE DEFINITION OF THE DEMOCRATIC IDEAL towards which we are./or ought to be aiming/striving for??!!!** Friends, is then not the right question to be asking ourselves?

First, tell u, I have boned up on American ??? history, especially their origin as an immigrant society "give us ur poor and huddled masses" that's the original message conveyed by the Statue of Liberty, i.e. America seen as a land of opportunity by immigrants from a Europe where class system prevailed and economy was over-populated so poor had not enough jobs/not enough to eat. I knew most of this already from my own studies of North American History by the author of the book: Industrialization and Economic History, J.R.T. Hughes, who described the origins and subsequent spread of the industrial modernization idea from its English birthplace, then to the northern countries of Europe, then to America which he described as the American

Offshoots. We needn't go into detail on this here, but he also described in detail what he termed "The European Take-Over Bid" of then primitive regions of the world, inhabited by self sufficient societies living in harmony with their environment and their neighbours, he caught the gist of the matter by saying "If there had been no missionaries..." would this world changing Take-Over Bid still have taken place in regions of Asia, Africa, and Latin America lasting approximately up and until regions won their independence most of them after WWII as a reward for being drafted into the Allied Powers war cause on account of their status as colonial protectorates. (Latin American

---

*   One of the obstacles to this ideal is the role that money plays in politics. To rectify this calls for financing political parties out of "public" rather than "private" funds so parties can compete on equal terms. ("level playing field").

Independence was gained a century earlier around 1848 as a result of Simon Bolivar's successful efforts to free Latin America of Spanish rulers).

Enough of historical background, and now on to some of the central issues facing North America at present and for the foreseeable future. First we state the problem, then we present our opinion as to the most promising solution(s). In this regard, I should mention, that while i am no expert from, most of my knowledge has been gained from reading Hillary Clinton's book: "Hard Choices", all about The Use of Smart Power in the Modern World*- and other than that just general knowledge garnered from magazines such as the London Economist while i still had subscription as well as books about America such as Francis Schaeffer's Christian book: How Should We Then Live? The Rise and Decline of Western Thought and Culture, in which he decries the absence of guiding moral principles to guide science and medicine (e.g. genetic engineering considered by him to be immoral, also being anti vivisection as being cruel to laboratory test animals, also too little regulation of potentially dangerous products such as pharmaceuticals which doctors tend to push on patients partly as a result of psychiatric community being beholden to pharmaceutical industry and vice versa). He also gazed into the crystal ball, predicting that growing shortages of energy and basic resources would undermine democratic institutions on account of federal government needing to impose sterner and sterner regulations on industry and possibly even rationing of essential resources among industrial users. To that list, we might add other issues that he did not foresee such as carbon/methane emissions leading to global weather warming and carbon tetraflourides from air-conditioning and dairy cow gas emissions leading to thinning of ozone layer and problem of ultra-violet rays reaching dangerous levels.

And of course the plunder of nature in the form of hunting down already scarce and disappearing species as well as the hope against hope last ditch efforts to ward off the lumbering interests so as to preserve the tropical rain forests and all other forests which serve as the lungs of the earth for all living/ breathing creatures. Enough said of these global problems. How to cope with them: clearly global problems call for a global response to them, i.e. all nations

---

*   On Canada, the book to read is "Canada After Harper, Stephen Harper's Ideologically Fuelled Attack on Traditional Canadian Society and Values. (Ed Finn/editor)

face up to crisis, and meet the challenge of unified global response to them. As I see it, that's a big part of the problem: when I was studying development economics during the height of the Cold War we had an English textbook, among others, that was called "A World Divided". As I said, that was at the height of the Cold War, long before the efforts of President Reagan and General Secretary Gorbachev to try and meet in the middle and more towards a "A Separate Peace" between their two countries. These two leaders achieved a great deal between them, the Berlin Wall fell, Germany was re-united on October 3, 1990, and Eastern Europe became independent of former Soviet influence which had dwindled to a very low level as a result of the widely acknowledged failures/shortcomings of the Gorbachev Economic Reforms.

Eventually, after former Sattelites departed from Soviet influence and their economies became models of competitive capitalism at its best (some of the older generation persons felt/still feel it would have been even better to combine the best of both worlds rather than throw out the whole kit and kaboodle where the old system was concerned) with many thriving small businesses and modern technology software producers, art, literature, and music thriving again free of censorship and meddling by the authorities). That basically brings us up to date. The world we live in is basically composed of diverse regional groupings whose cooperation will all be required if we are to successfully face up to and effectively resolve the serious problems facing the planet in unison. While one nation can take the lead, no nation alone can resolve the problems facing the planet, it will take the cooperation of all concerned. Hence the title of this book: "Adaptations: The Potential of Competitive Capitalism the World Over to Adapt to Changing Economic, Technological, Social, Political, and Ecological Conditions in the 21ˢᵗ Century". Everyone these days being familiar with the theory (whether guided by God or not) of Evolution, u will recall that success of any species depends not only on its ability to prevail over, but also, even more, on its ability to adapt and live together in harmony with other species sharing the same, for want of a better word, call it "living space", which is the same things as saying we share living space on a not very large, becoming more over-crowded every decade, roundish sphere known as planet earth. I am aware of efforts to colonize Mars and find new "lebensraum" (pardon the expression) but personally I do not think these efforts stand very much greater prospects of success, at least not for the average income individual, than Hitler despot's attempt to secure his so-called "lebensraum" in the lands to the east of Germany during WWII - the only difference being that whereas the lands to the east were only thinly settled the lands on Mars are without any kind of settlement.

So, where does all this discussion of planetary problems lead us. Well, as Reagan would start his sentences, let's see: First we have identified the main challenges facing the planet and those of us living on it. To repeat: the first and foremost problem is the world divided aspect. When the world is divided and nations see each other as competitors for strategic interests such as oil, control of economy, and trade, instead of partners aiming to face up to and successfully cope with global challenges in unison rather than divided. This brings us to the central theme of this book: peace is the essential need and spells victory/enables the essential victory of the people's of the world/ over and against the divisive forces of national rivalries and competitions over strategic interests and power over/rather than power with/others. Before moving along to a discussion of domestic policy issues, invite everyone to join me in searching Google for three most magnificent songs inspiring people and, possibly also leaders, to seek peace:

1) first song: Burning Heart (Survivor)
2) second song: The Victory is Peace (1972 Sapporo Olympics theme song) (John Denver, Tracy Nivert, and Bill Dannoff)
3) third song: Peace on Earth Good Will towards Men (Casting Crowns).

After we have taken a short breather, we may be able to tackle the problem of domestic issues facing the North American Economy. But, at this moment just sit back and enjoy listening to this inspiring music and its message to leaders and citizens of North America alike/both. That's what I am going to do, I will store this email in Drafts and hope i don't lose it/will be able to retrieve it, give myself say 20 minutes restful music to gather my strength/muster my reserves of energy before resuming the conversation.

For those of u who are older persons such as myself (61 3/4 and counting) I will avoid getting myself too hyper-emotional and will listening to "cool down" music on apple iTunes as I always do to get the adrenaline back to normal after listening to motivational/emotional music such as the three masterpieces listed above. So for me it's going to be "calming music for dogs" previewed on apple iTunes accessed by typing that into the Google Search Bar, u should see a golden retriever on ur screen and a playlist of some 20 instrumental pieces being previewed - unfortunately the length of each preview has come down from 3:00 minutes to only 0.30 minutes but u can always proceed to the next melody, indeed the laptop sometimes graces u by doing that automatically. Bye for now (1140 hrs. Ottawa time). Catch u again around 1200 hrs. Ottawa time. Guess I'll have to postpone lunch at least until 1300 hrs. it seems. Bye for now, dear reader:

Hi,

Back again. Apologize for taking so long (almost an hour longer than expected) it took some time to get the PSW's at my retirement home to bring a tray with my midday meal (made up of veggie quiche, white toast, and to drink orange juice, milk, and coffee, as requested, upon reflection i notice now that they did not bring coffee, made conspicuous by its absence as the saying goes). On top of that the cat (his name, it's Birdy) was out of sorts and not settling down as his his wont, and me feeling a bit zerstraut (that's german: for frazzled nerves on account of the likewise mood of the cat). Well realizing that he needed to fortify himself he called down to nurse Jenny to hurry up and bring Underdog (Chris) his special "Energy Pill" which she did, earlier than usual, 1:00 p.m., instead of the usual 3:00 p.m. Well, now with his special "Energy Pill" he senses that he is stronger again and feeling that he now has the motivation and energy to complete the rest of the thoughts he wishes to express in this "open letter to the public": Thank u once again for willingness to be captive audience, and now it's high time we be getting on with the rest of this email.

1) What to do About Social Policy

First off we come to the thorny issue of social policy. Being no expert on either Canadian, and even less so, on American social policies. I will limit myself to offering a suggestion for a social security system developed by Milton Friedmann which he offered as a substitute for all other forms of social security such as government health insurance and accident insurance plans, unemployment insurance and workmen's compensation (in Canada), and child benefit allowances (once again in Canada) and veteran's affairs. Not being an expert or trained in social policy (although I am trained/college educated (Master's in Economic Science) as well as largely Self Educated across a broader spectrum/range than what I got in college. for example in all my five years of study, only one course on Canadian Economy per se (the first year paperback by Ian Drummond which was far from sufficient background to help me succeed in the federal government's most powerful ministry, i took courses in college named "Canadian Economy" but learned nothing about the Canadian whatsoever from Richardson's esoteric book "Regional Economic Theory" all about "circles representing autonomous regional space" invented by somebody or other (Ah! ya! I believe August Loesch was the name) I did remember his name, was going to say Euclid for Euclidean spaces, but that being good stuff is not to be confused with the theoretical irrellevant stuff I learned in that paperback by Harry Richardson, nice intellectual exercise for theoretically minded, of no relevance to policy in the real world of Canadian economy, which I only much later learned, from a book by a Swedish lady at Ryerson Polytechnic by the name of Ingrid Bryan named: Economic Policies in Canada. There I learned everything I needed to know, I was now all dressed up in finery with nowhere to go after my breakdown when i became a real outcast/pariah from respectable society at alma mater and elsewhere. Ah! Now I Remember: All the English History I Need to Know, that's great stuff, i mean rather the name of another author whose name eludes my memory, thinking... maybe it will come to me...

Back to Friedmann's proposal for a blanket scheme of social assistance, which is none other than his renowned proposed system for:

A Negative Income Tax

Sounds complicated but it's really not, it's quite simple to understand in essence.

Wish me luck in explaining. First step is the government sets a target for a base level of social assistance that everyone gets when he is out of work beyond a certain length of time for any reason whatsoever to provide that person with his basic needs for food, clothing, and housing. In popular folklore, u'll no doubt recall the stereotypical image of the "lazy bum" "who won't get off his f*****ing ass" and pay his way/pull his weight in life, just sits around all day collecting welfare benefits and watching television all day when he's not drinking alcohol, snorting crack, or smoking cigarettes non-stop all of which are covered by his welfare benefits for social parasite; as in all generalizations there is an element of truth as well a hefty dose of exaggeration/tarring all welfare recipients with the same brush. In fact, welfare recipients can be broken down into two different classes:

1) those persons who are unable to work
2) those persons who are unwilling to work

Broadly speaking, Friedman felt, the first class of persons has every right to protected by a social safety net if he is unable to work by reason of permanent or temporary disability, or he is unable to work by reason of pregnancy, or by reason of insufficient employment opportunities because of recession or declining industries, or because person is a member of any minority being discriminated against in their search for employment. In this regard i just can't resist referencing u to a very catchy/funny song by singer/songwriter Big Bill Broonzy to be found on the album: Big Bill Broonzy, Pioneer of the Blues which can be accessed on utube. Actually i was the proud owner of one of his LP's (long playing records, that are just now again coming into fashion on account of their inspiring covers compared to the newer CD's (compact discs) which had replaced them for a while on the market).

The Lyrics to Pioneer of the Blues are very simple and easy to memorize: Broonzy repeats them in several different contexts ranging from the local employment office to waiting for drinks to be served at a local bar, to being paid equal amount for equal work as whites and others. I will repeat only the refrain accompanying each situation and it is memorable:

if u white,
it's alright!

if u brown,
stick around!

but if u black,
oh! brother!
get back!
get back!
get back!

I hope i made u smile/not scowl with this little imagery.

Now to "get back" to Friedman's blanket all under one umbrella covered, Negative Income Tax. To what and to whom does it apply? It applies to the class of persons who are receiving social assistance by reason of unwillingness/ not inability to work. He does not present any data on the relative size of the two groups as percentage of total welfare recipients, but it can be assumed that he is addressing primarily/exclusively that group of welfare recipients who are unwilling to work/not unable to. (in other words those referred to disparagingly by conservatives as "lazy bums" whereas leftists in Canada have been known to even the score by referring to "corporate welfare bums" who receive all kinds of tax break/do not pay their fair share of income tax on account of loopholes which conservative economists euphemistically refer to as "tax expenditures", meaning money that is lost to the government classed as expenditure by the government - I wonder what position the tax collector would take on that, wouldn't the IRS/Revenue Canada tend to view so-called tax expenditures as loopholes whereby the already swimming in profits corporations avoid paying their fair share in taxes to the government. What this amounts to is that the nominal tax rates documented in the government's account book differ greatly from the actual tax rates in the account books of the more profitable of the corporations. In popular parlance this is referred to as "keeping two sets of books" one for show only, the other for real deal/bad deal for democratically well run government and those average citizens who are the major beneficiaries of government programs in the nation. Eliminating tax loopholes and making corporations as well as wealthy individuals pay their fair share in taxes (either through proportional taxation as in America or slightly progressive taxation as to in Canada, either way fair is fair if they are supposed to pay 30% in income taxes announced to the public on election day only fair that they don't pay less due to fancy loopholes and other devious methods (leave them unnamed).

Having said all that what is the merit/demerit of Friedmann's Negative Income Tax, known as the NIT to economists? It is that it builds incentives to work into the welfare system that motivates those able to work/return to work to part with only a smaller proportion of their welfare benefits than the additional income they receive from gainful employment. For example: say u have a welfare recipient who can earn $ 15/hr. (minimum wage in Canada

I believe)** from returning to work, but loses the equivalent of $ 15/hr. in welfare benefits if accepts said gainful employment. What incentive does the welfare recipient have to return to work when he can receive the same amount of money without having to work for it/do his own thing so to speak back home in his apartment?

Friedmann's NIT Scheme would ensure that for each $ 15/hr received from gainful employment, a lesser amount than the full $ 15/hr or equivalent would be lost in welfare benefits. The less the loss in welfare benefits the greater the incentive to seek/search for work/gainful employment - simple but effective way of building monetary incentives into the welfare system which have got a terrible reputation precisely because they discourage people from wanting to work/fail to provide them with monetary motivation to search for employment/return to work. How does Friedmann envisage his scheme being put into practice by governments? The negative income tax seems to refer to granting tax relief on total income in declining proportion as income from gainful employment rises. At low levels of employment income, the tax relief is largest to provide maximum incentive to get out into the workforce again, which can be quite traumatic for anyone who has been out of work for any length of time, there is a social stigma attached not only to being on "pogey" but also to having had to rely on "pogey". Which type of welfare scheme is less costly/less drain on the government? Clearly Friedmann's. Apart from having to pay out less in welfare benefits to those individuals who get off the welfare rolls and onto the employment rolls, the government potentially benefits from those on employment rolls now paying higher income tax. This would potentially more than offset the loss in tax revenue from granting tax relief to those still receiving welfare. Why have not more government's adopted Friedmann's proposed Negative Income Tax (NIT)? That I don't know, perhaps one drawback from the point of the government bureaucracy is that by streamlining/simplifying the system there is less need for bureaucrats/civil servants as opposed to to systems involving a multiplicity of programs, e.g. a separate program for each type of need, whether it be disability benefits, health benefits, accident benefits, veterans' benefits, pregnant mothers' benefits, daycare allowances and what have u/and so on and so forth. This brings us to a real limitation of Friedman's NIT if

---

*   In the states, the minimum wage averages around $ 7/hr although with variations
     from state to state.

and only if it becomes an umbrella substitute/replacement for all these other much needed programs which differentiate according to type of need. But if it is applied alone to social assistance for those receiving standard welfare benefits not covered by any of these other programs, it would seem to be a step in the right direction toward modernizing standard base line social assistance by building in incentives to search for/return to work. To that extent we/i can highly recommend adopting Friedman's NIT.

What order of magnitude benefit can be expected from adopting it. Seeing that it is primarily beneficial to the government in relation to the proportion of persons able but unwilling to work as a proportion of the total size of the population receiving any kind of welfare from any of the various programs currently in place/on offer. That is something requiring further research by myself and/or u, the reader. My guess is that it might apply to about 25% of the total population on welfare, correct me if I'm wrong.

A complementary way to increase incentives to work is by raising the minimum wage which applies across a wide range of occupations ranging from waiters and waitresses, to bartenders, to meter maids and parking attendants, to office clerks and secretaries, to receptionists working in dental and medical offices, hotels and restaurants, and so on and so forth. Economists sometimes argue that minimum wages that price workers above the equilibrium level that would otherwise be prevailing on account of supply and demand/price the least skilled workers out of jobs by reducing the demand for labour below the available supply of workers creating excess supply of labour often known also as disincentive to hire employment. How great this disincentive effect is depends on many things such as whether demand curve is downward sloping (usually taken for granted by conservative economists, they go to great lengths to prove that this must be the case by inventing various theories of the demand curve under differing assumptions about the type of market, the type of product, and the type of consumer (how rational is he, does he always comparison shop, my mother drove my father into rages because she was not very good at comparison shopping for groceries even though the grocery bill never was excessive in relation to the high income my father made as a LCOL in the military, spent mostly on fancy cars and boats for himself which he wanted more than us/all we wanted mom/me was a bit of tender loving care but he just wasn't the type!). Well to get back to the point I am trying to make, what if demand curve for some occupations is not downward sloping but constant level because of inflexible needs for particular services? For example, a given community of certain population size will need only so many barbers, only so many hairdressers, only so many gas station attendants, only so many cashiers at so many supermarkets, so lowering the wage beneath the government stipulated (a la conservative minimum wage - haters) does not in this case increase employment but only hurts incomes of those already employed.

Conclusion for Improving Social Policy

1) recommend adoption of Friedmann's Negative Income Tax (NIT) for standard welfare benefits not covered by/under any of other existing specialized programs for particular groups. Retain these other programs in addition to Friedmann's.

2) recommend raising the minimum wage to cover a large proportion of workers providing essential services to the community that no one else wants to do on account of the exceptional disutility from working in these Cinderella on her knees scrubbing floors type occupations and/or trades. Because such a large proportion of the total labour force is engaged in working at such occupations (this is again something needing further research but as a rough guess i would put the figure at around 40% of the total labour force, it is a well known fact that relatively very few people in society are able to finance or cope with getting a college degree, yet the so-called "rights and privileges" associated with such degrees entitle holders to an inordinate income for no other reason that they hold this degree (not that the work they perform is more needed/nor because their productivity is higher in terms of what they actually produce in the form of goods and services). Therefore recommend raising the minimum wage to the extent desired/deemed fair/without pricing workers out of markets.

1) What to Do About the Twin Problems of Recession, Increased Deficit Spending, and Rising Burden of Interest on Debt Owed by Households to Banks for Mortgages and by Government to Households on Account of Fiscal Stimulus/Deficit Spending

When an economy is in recession, there is no longer full employment (full employment is generally taken to be around 5% rate of unemployment to allow for frictional unemployment that is temporary unemployment representing persons moving between/from one job to another because they want to/not because they can't find work).

When the level of employment falls the government generally feels obligated to increase its own spending on goods and services as a counterweight to the loss of spending on the part of households either because household members are unemployed or can find only part time contract work. But any policy to increase spending to stimulate demand in the economy (known as "fiscal stimulus") will increase the government deficit by raising government expenditures higher than the government's tax intake. At the same time as government expenditures are increasing, the government's intake in tax revenues will generally be falling on account of unemployed persons detracting from the size of the sum total of incomes (GDP) generated in the economy depending largely on the total number of persons who are unemployed. When unemployment goes up, government tax revenue goes down given constant rates of taxation at each level of personal income. What we have established so far is that both lower tax intake due to lower GDP as well as the fiscal stimulus governments' provide to increase demand in the economy to/and put people back to work, both of these factors increase the size of the government's deficit - the government deficit being the difference between the government's total expenditures and the government's total tax revenues.

If government tax revenues do not cover the costs of government expenditures how on earth does the government finance the excess of expenditures over and above available tax revenues? Answer: it borrows money from private firms and private households by the sale of fixed interest government bonds and or treasury bills. On occasion it resorts to just printing more paper which passes for more purchasing power/consumer demand only as long as more money chasing fewer goods does not lead to inflation of prices which of course means that consumers' purchasing power/and real GDP, has not risen at all, or even, fallen. For this reason, printing money is often referred to as "fiscal irresponsibility" and governments tend to disfavour printing money if they can borrow the money instead.

Effect of Recession and Deficit Spending on the Domestic Debt and Interests Payments Thereon Crowding Out Sorely Needed Expenditures on Existing and Planned Government Programs such as Health, Education and Welfare (mainly pensions)

We have seen that recession, combined with deficit spending leads to an increase in the overall level of the money owed by the government to firms and households: in other words in the overall level of the domestic government debt both absolutely and as a proportion of Gross Domestic Product (GDP). With rising level of debt of course comes rising burden of interest payments on the government as it pays out interest from its available tax revenue intake/ instead of being able to devote the tax revenues to existing, potentially and actually, much needed government programs leading to cutbacks in essential services such as the mails the number of nurses in hospitals, the number of teachers in schools and the number of $$$ available for welfare (esp. old age pensions), and unemployment insurance.

So the ratio of debt to GDP is a very important barometer of an economy's overall health, this applies also to debt owed to foreign countries when our country sells less to other countries than other countries sell to us.

To finance the difference in sales, to/and purchases from, domestic companies and individuals desiring foreign goods will be forced to borrow foreign exchange from other countries who only accept payment in their own currency for the obvious reason, that they have no reason to want excess of our currency when they have no need/desire to buy more goods/services from us. During a recession, because of lower incomes on the part of our firms and households, we tend to buy less from other countries while other countries buy the same amount from us unless they too are suffering from a recession. In a well established free trading multilateral trading system there are a number of especially dangerous pitfalls/wrong government policies can produce/lead to:

-   thinking that the cupboard is bare of revenues already, governments' may be loathe to provide needed stimulus to the economy (a la Keynes, the premier-exponent of deficit spending during recession and surplus spending during the next boom (assuming it eventuates), which evens out both the deficit and the debt level over time and is therefore the responsible course of action by governments wanting stability in the economy above all else (as opposed to recklessly spending more and more on government programs even during times of booms when they should be repaying the debt accumulated 1.) from the last recession). I.e. the pitfall of "fiscal irresponsibility".

- thinking that they can increase demand for their own products 2.) through "beggar thy neighbour" policies governments may resort to raising tariffs, devaluing their currencies, and/or imposing foreign exchange controls - limiting access to government's foreign exchange reserves is done to limit the amount of goods that firms and households can buy from foreign countries.

- the problem with these "beggar thy neighbour" policies is that they lead to "retaliatory" beggar thy neighbour policies from other countries resulting that they all cancel each other's benefits out, but that's not all. With all countries importing less and less from other countries/each other, the overall spending/demand in the world/international economy goes on a downward spiral which benefits no-one and harms everyone.

* - A Policy of Voluntary Wage Restraint Helps Boost Employment as Well as Saving the Government Money (perhaps combined with a cut in sales taxes to boost consumer demand to create demand for the newly re-employed workers/at the lower wages so firms do not lose out on market demand on account of lower wages.

It behooves us all to learn from past experience, since past experience is our guide for the future, and can prevent us from repeating past mistakes. In this regard it should be noted that the above described risky policies or policy pitfalls were to a large extent responsible for the Worldwide Great Depression that hit the Capitalist World in 1939 and lasted in almost all cases in 1939 (Nazi Germany was an exception their buildup of infrastructure (e.g. autobahn highways (not "high way") networks to ferry troops to all extremities/borders of the nation/combined with rapid secret rearmament going on inside Germany's munitions factories and emphasis on self suffiency in strategic resources need in wartime counteracted the effects of the depression on demand much in the way Keynes described in his book "The General Theory of Employment, Interest, and Money". However this book being very technical and based on not easy for any intelligent laymen to understand/decipher. A better choice would be the book by the renowned Canadian author, Pierre Berton (Hero), entitled simply as follows: The Great Depression 1929-1939. Although this book is with special reference to Canada, the broader causes, consequences, and side effects of the great depression are not at all left out of account. This is THE book to read to understand what/what not to do when depression looms on the horizon. I highly recommend Pierre Berton (Hero) authored book to anyone wishing to understand the root causes, consequences. side effects, and policy remedies for.

Conclusions on How to Respond to Looming Recession

1)   Firstly, we avoid the pitfalls listed above: "beggar thy neighbour" policies which in no small part aggravated/exacerbated the depression/made it worse rather than better/.

2)   Secondly, governments that are already saddled with very high debt burdens (both domestic and foreign debt ratios are very high), should think twice about engaging in too much further deficit spending which will only aggravate/exacerbate the problem of excessive debt, its bad consequences, and its risky side effects. Resist the temptation to boost internal demand through arms/military buildup/investment in arms yields no $$$ return on investment. There are other ways to stimulate demand than military buildups which lead to widespread paranoia on the part of rivals and counterpoint military buildups which could possibly lead to world becoming another "powder keg" waiting to explode as it ended up doing just that/at the time of WWI breakout/breakdown of peace in 1914. Avoid repeating the mistake of the Kaiser who was so rigid in his ways that he was unable to register alarm bells which should have been sounding in his head as warning to back off/change course/do 180 degree turnabout. He should immediately have been given tranquillizers to calm his mind down and enable him to think rationally at this decisive moment of crisis situation.

Had anyone thought to do this - put him on a good tranquillizer - to make any person calm down yet not be zombie but be able to think logically and lucidly and above all tremulously, The rational human being has rational responses to whatever stimuli enter his mind. Consider the stimulus/rational response to "fear": Rational, meaning that when a man is afraid he asks himself how do I avoid whatever is the source of his fear from hurting him/giving the source of the fear a chance to hurt him. A rational response to fear is to pull back, exercise caution, try to prevent anything bad from happening to oneself. An irrational response to fear is to dig in one's heels, allow oneself to be provoked into an angry/angrier/angriest state in which one does the very thing that brings on the things any rational person wishes to avoid: bringing hurt upon himself and those around him.

Unfortunately for Germany, the Kaiser responded to fear in just such an irrational manner as described above.

At the very time he should have been hearing those alarm bells going off inside his brain/seeing red flags going up before his eyes warning him to back away from his self destructive course...well, to make a long story short, he foolishly spoke/uttered the words that cast the die in favour of war..."full steam ahead"... What can we learn from this? First of all, from among the possible candidates running for election we choose one who exhibits greatest wisdom/prudence/ responsible behaviour. And if we happen to be saddled with a clone of the Kaiser, who was an emotional/blustering/red faced type of individual we make sure that someone makes him takes good tranquillizers best suited to helping him think calmly and rationally (not fogging his mind even more or jangling/ firing up his raw nerves even more) and thus able to know what to do/what not to do when faced with a crisis of the kind that faced the Kaiser...

Realize this about a red faced/blustering/emotional individual: Red face is less of a threat than white face always. Red face is angry man/white man is full of blind unreasoning hatred. Red face can still be reached with the help of the right tranquilizers and persuasion...

Now I will pause with my email and save my further ideas for another day(s) and another email(s)...Til then! Chris).

P.S. To end on a positive note/footing how about we listen to some really great music to inspire us onward and upward to better things/better future...

1) Man in the Mirror (Michael Jackson)
2) Ebony and Ivory (Paul McCartney/Stevie Wonder)
3) Joe Turner (Big Bill Broonzy)
4) The Tolerance Song (Checker and the Bluetones)
5) What the World Needs Now (Jackie de Shannon)
6) Peace Train (Cat Stevens)
7) I Heard the Bells on Christmas Day (Johnny Reid/et, al.)

Adaptations (Part 2 Of 2)

Hi! My name is Chris. I am college- and self-educated: I have a knack for summarizing lengthy and complicated books in a few pages of typewritten notes: economic and cultural history, the world wars, classical literature, the realities of the world, both rich and poor, philosophy, some psychology (relationships), three languages, the dictionary, the encyclopedia, basic knowledge about medicine and our bodies, as well as the contemporary political scene from an American perspective. I have written 6 serious books (including some very interesting (to me) revisions of my college essays) along with 3 small happy books of poems that i would some day like to see published in part or in whole. I wrote 2 original books updating both poor and rich country economics for the 21st century based on my researches; also a book of poems called "ideas of ten great economic thinkers in perspective" from Adam Smith, through Malthus, Ricardo, and Friedman. As well as a book delving into German, Canadian, as well as world, cultural and political history. In other words circumstances led to me becoming a freelance writer. I believe I have written not great quantity, but quality. I have also written some very interesting (to me) essays including an essay on the positive theory of democracy developed by economists, comparing it to the older normative approach of the classical writers. As well as critically examined state of the art, unorthodox applications of economic theory, such as the economic approach to human behaviour. Lastly, I have written/published a happy book of poems called "A Single Rose Can be My Garden: My First Pet, A Penny For Your Thoughts, Gently Down the Stream, Everything under the sun" available online from various sellers...If u should get around to reading it, I hope u will find some things u like within its pages...! (cover design not my precise choice!). Why am i on this dating site, u may ask? Anastasiadate sent me ur beautiful/lovely pics/profiles which I, as a citizen of the world, i was/am very gratified to receive. ur chris)

> "We have a small house dog named Winston, I believe he was named after me/yours truly -

> Joke of the Day:
> Q: - Is Winston a danger to society?
>   - Or is society a danger to Winston?

> A: All Winston did was "bark" a lil angrily in his own bedroom way back when. Never did he "bite" anybody or anything. If, in fact, there are any "victims of dog bites" please look elsewhere than Winston...!

North American Society, like Northern European Society was founded on two basic ideas: the idea of not only Political Freedom (the opposite of political dictatorship) but the Christian Idea of Compassion (which is the opposite of cruelty). Most of what is wrong with this, our world, has to do with cruelty winning the day over the principle of compassion. To take just one example (others include the evils of war (especially unnecessary ones) and the evils of the strong exploiting the weak rather than protecting them): witness the cruel treatment of inmates/patients in dungeons and dragons type prisons and mental hospitals. If I was king/president for a day what I would do is to reform the prison and the hospital system, with the aim of giving the less well endowed and the less fortunate members of society with a half way decent life, by/thru providing them with more lebensraum (german: living space). In other words, I would build rehabilitation centres and mental health centres. Set an example to the whole word that we North Americans are anything but a "lock up" society. Being a society founded and still to great extent true to its Christian principles. My slogan as as president for a day would be: we can do better/let's set an example to the world by getting our own house in order before we tell others to get theirs in order. On issues of domestic policy it puts forth incentive providing welfare system, recommends an increase in the minimum wage which applies to up to 40% of the labour force (we vigorously dispute the claim of conservative economists that increasing the minimum wage prices low skilled workers out of jobs on account of demand being fixed by set/fixed needs for particular classes of workers). On combatting recession,

I propose that the government makes an appeal to private enterprises in the best interests of the country that they apply the brakes/ cut back on wages and salaries, so that with given budget of enterprise can afford to hire/more employees to reach full employment without going the present route of more and more fiscal stimulus through ever greater deficits adding to spiralling domestic indebtedness with interest payments crowding out more and more needed government programs and threatening default. The advantage of my approach is that it achieves the same result of full employment without the government having to spend/waste so much money on fiscal stimulus in times of recession. Currently the leading sector in Canada is comprised of exports of oil (reserves are running out except very costly oil extracted from the Alberta Tar Sands). Next to exporting oil (instead of conserving it for own use) we also export a wide range of unfinished and semi finished goods, i.e. raw materials such as metals and minerals from the Canadian Shield to the north. My suggestion is to keep exporting these materials but to first add value to them through processing the outputs and producing the inputs. Our manufacturing sector, in common with America is, as a result of robot technology automation displacing blue collar workers on a grand scale as well as overall demand shifting more to post industrial service sector composed of firms producing goods for leisure uses such as grocery stores clothing stores, fast food restaurants, hotels, sporting goods, as well as higher skilled manpower requiring software producing small niche companies We keep this sector "as is" on account of being the home of a great proportion of the work force. Technology Intensive Sector: the world and domestic markets being super competitive and hard to successfully break into until recently we were in last position among the OECD capitalist countries. This sector, almost universally regarded as a panacea, answer to all our problems. I beg to disagree especially in the our case where the domestic tech companies are swallowed up by American takeovers before they even mature, venture capital from start to completion is notoriously difficult/to obtain at reasonable rates. Again: this rat race sector where old products are quickly obsolete necessitating a constant drive to move on to ever newer products and markets (this is well known fact first pointed out by the great economic thinker, Schumpeter, with his product S curve cycle with high growth as new product enters, market later to decline as markets dwindle on account of newer competing technologies making initial product obsolete not even mentioned by neoclassical school prevailing in north american universities Shumpeter's ideas need to be added when it comes to high tech. The EPA (the recently dismantled Environmental

Protection Agency) forecast that even if we replaced all fossil fuels on which industry is currently 95% dependent the mere fact that dairy animals release so many greenhouse gases into the atmosphere, means that we will exceed our safe limit for those gases by the calendar year 2030! That's only twelve years from now. How much will that date move forward if we don't eliminate that other 50% of greenhouse gasses produced by fossil fuel depending industry? Back in 1977, the MIT Limits to Growth predicted that by 2020 resource shortages, population growth and industrial growth would interact in such a way as to produce a collapse not only in the global ecosphere but in global food production creating a planetary chaos. I am not someone who revels in theories of doomsday to back up any unproven theories in books on religion, I am a scientist who extrapolates current trends into the future and tries to analyze their effects on the global balance between demands on/available supplies of resources of arable land, ocean fish stocks, and demands on the environment (e.g. global weather warming and weather extremes which do not bode well for crops luscious and green). If u want to ameliorate the situation u do it by putting in place wise policies after first facing up to any and all problems, This will involve teamwork between the nations where each nation does its part/it's duty. But are nations doing this? In fact just the opposite! Nations are showing themselves from their worst sides, once again engaging in armaments buildups leading to an atmosphere not entirely unlike that which prevailed prior to the to the outbreak of prior to outbreak of WWI where opposing alliances had manoeuvred themselves into a position from which it was hard to escape. The "powder keg" that eventually blew up in the faces of all of all the participants regardless of which alliance/side they belonged to.

So what are the challenges/changing conditions presently facing Canadian democracy/competitive capitalism?

And what is the best way to adapt to them? Friends: is that not the right question to be asking ourselves? Differing schools of thoughts have differing answers, but all have to deal with changing conditions/changing challenges ahead: changing conditions relating to the earth's ecology/differing views of severity of and appropriate response to/the limits to growth and whether and how to respond/displacement of workers by automation and whether and how to respond/democratic management of the economy without adding to the debt a controversial issue/differing views on the need for regulation in relation to everything/itself a problem/differing views on the role of democratically well run government/itself a problem.

The major challenges ahead/what are they?/any list would have to include the following: outdated (or anachronistic) energy technologies (those that contribute to climate change)/outdated concepts of progress (demanding more and more material wealth at a time when the carrying capacity of the planet is already being stretched to the breaking point)/outdated ways of managing the economy (piling up debt instead of living within our means through voluntary wage restraint)/outdated hatred of any and all regulation (as infringement on enterprise freedom to plunder nature/pollute the environment)/outdated hatred of any and all government (just get the government off the backs of the people and all will be well (meaning the upper income strata/echelons/what has this led to if not the public sector being starved of resources and shortages of essential services provided by nurses and teachers/hospitals and schools)// too much top talent devoted to producing pollution intensive products, i.e. building ever more cars/ever more planes/ever more armaments/that lead only to roads that are congested/skies that are overcrowded/and hate and suspicion between countries/everyone wants to rule the world but what has arms buildup actually achieved if not just a "stalemate in hostility"/in peace there is not weakness but strength at a time when global challenges require/ call for global responses (top engineering talent might better be deployed toward the great task of energy technology conversion from non renewable/ polluting tech/to renewable clean tech/pollution abatement/and clean up after ourselves technologies.

There are two stereotypes/bogeymen images of the North American economy/ both of which stand in the way of finding common solutions to the common problems facing us today: a) the image of an economy being strangled to death in a web of government red tape/all regulation as an infringement on enterprise freedom including those which prohibit plunder of nature/ and freedom to pollute/and protect the worker and the consumer (i.e. the government as the villain and root of all evil in our economy) b) the image of an economy run by greedy corporations who use workers only/solely for the purpose of squeezing out maximum profits for the corporation/there is no such thing as shared interests/the idea that the prosperity of the enterprise is the prosperity of both workers and management they cast out the window (i.e. the corporate bloodsuckers/as the villain and root of all evil in our economy).

Why do they stand in the way of us finding common solutions to the common problems we face, u ask? Let's just say: the more time and energy we waste on fighting our ideological opponents, the less time and energy we will have left over to devote to finding common solutions to common problems. The man whose thinking is ruled/dominated by ideological stereotypes will, like Don Quixote, devote all his time and energy to battling ideological windmills on the opposing side of the political spectrum. Oh! If only we could get rid/replace all government? Oh! If only we could get rid of/replace all corporations? Those are the rallying battle cries of the ideological warriors on both the Right as well as the Left...All we can say is that in an age when we all of us together face common challenges wouldn't be better to say united we stand divided we fall, which is another way of saying: the interests of the whole, shouldn't they be placed above narrow partisan interests in gaining a larger slice of the economic pie for ourselves??!!!

That's really what left and right are all about: under the guise of preaching salvation for our society and the world, they are really just rationalizing getting a larger slice of the political and economic pie/for themselves. In my humble opinion, we should not be focussing on this zero sum game of take from my neighbour so I can have more, but be focussing on how we can enlarge/improve the quality of life in our society and on our planet for both us AND our neighbour. That's not socialism/that is Christianity/the Christian Idea! Love thy neighbour as thyself. Shall we all raise a glass to it? Amen. (I agree).

Best regards,
Chris Nelson),

Post Script 1: Climate Change - Making the 2030 Time Line for 'Reversibility'

There are basically two ways to reduce climate change carbon dioxide/methane (greenhouse) emissions to the required level by 2030 - to prevent climate change from becoming irreversible - going past the point of no return. The first, much talked about, but little acted upon, way/method is to:

a) convert as many existing greenhouse polluting industries as amenable away from greenhouse fossil fuels to other energy technologies, above all traditional hydroelectric power - THE BACKBONE of any renewable energy strategy identified by the original 1990 Brundtland Report, entitled Our Common Future - as well to non traditional more costly, solar, wind power, and tidal power, i.e. the fancier, costlier, to develop/disseminate stuff.

The second, less talked about, maybe not even though of way/method for cutting down/back on carbon dioxide/methane pollution is to:

b) re-orient production ITSELF, away from greenhouse polluting sectors by reallocating productive resources, - i.e. capital, labour, natural resources and energy inputs - toward other non greenhouse producing sectors (such as those foreseen in the book that accurately predicted the trend toward the -"The Post- Industrial Society". The basic argument outlined in this book was that because of trends in supply -automation displacing workers in traditional manufacturing- as well as the trend in consumer demand increasingly towards the service sector, both of these factors would contribute to an increase in the relative size of the latter and decline in the relative size of the former, in terms of both output and employment, esp, the latter. What is the relevance of all this to climate change u ask? Well, we were talking about re-orienting production away from greenhouse polluting industries towards non-greenhouse polluting sectors, weren't we? Well, there u have it: underlying trends in the economy already go part way to achieving that aim/goal. Part way? I'm making the assumption that we can accellerate that existing trend - ride on that wave -through putting in place the right mix of policies, so as to better assure ourselves of reaching those critical target levels of lower greenhouse emissions by the target date of 2030. By what means can this be done, u ask? Well, the traditional method of encouraging "merit industries" and discouraging "demerit industries" has been through the use of financial incentives and disincentives, which take the form of subsidies and taxes. (take cigarettes and high tech - cigarettes were often discouraged/ taxed on account of being believed to be dangerous to one's health/high tech encouraged by means of subsidies for firms conducting meritorious research.) FIRMS ARE THEREBY PROVIDED WITH AN INCENTIVE TO AVOID THE TAX BY INSTALLING GREENHOUSE POLLUTION ABATEMENT EQUIPMENT/

Accompanying financial support, came sometimes also direct investment and manpower planning, such as the creation of Petro Canada as a window on the oil industry and a flagship in the search for new oil reserves in the Canada Lands. All the above policies have at one time been tried in Canada (e.g. financial incentives/disincentives, direct investment (crown corporations/ TransMountain Pipeline) and manpower planning (Eastern Offshore). Much depends on their political acceptability given the particular government and party in power, and the prevailing/ruling economic ideas, whether they be leaning to the right, the middle, or the left. But sometimes political pragmatism calls for parties to forget their ideological leanings and tackle common problems with common solutions - i.e. to place the welfare of the whole above their narrow partisan interests. So far we have established that it might not be a bad idea to accellerate the existing trend in the economy towards the service sector on account that this might help us achieve our greenhouse emissions reduction goals. So what is the shape of The Post Industrial Society: computer software companies, diversified organic agriculture (as opposed to pesticide using soya and corn for processed foods), reforestation and saving the Amazon Rainforest (if necessary through compensation), re-stocking the oceans with fish, taking plastic pollutants out of the ocean depths, high tech garbage disposal (recycling) sites away from floating rafts of garbage into the oceans and rivers, creation of nature reserves and nature parks, as well as promoting development of the energy technologies, the pollution abatement technologies, and the clean up after ourselves (e.g. The Great Lakes) technologies of the future,. There is enormous employment potential in the above three sectors (so says the London Economist), Other sectors envisaged for the Post Industrial Society, include leisure based service industries such as hotels, restaurants, sporting goods, clothing, footwear, movie theatres, events (such as sports and concerts), increased resources toward improving education and health care, improved social services for the homeless, battered women, children, youth, addictions, public transit, taxis (e.g. Uber), delivery, retirement homes, low income housing, longer unpaid vacations and more leisure so that firms with a given budget can afford to employ more people. This last recommendation provides a possible way to have full employment without the need for eternal/everlasting growth placing ever greater/growing demands on the fragile environment/ecosystem of the planet not to mention finite supplies of natural resources.

Comparing method (a) with method (b) above, what can we say about their relative efficacy/feasibility:

- method (a) alone, according to the former Environmental Protection Agency (EPA), would cost no less than a whopping 47 trillion dollars and would take 20 years to implement, longer than the time line of 2030 gives us to meet our emmission reduction goals/targets.

- method (b), by contrast would just involve, at a minimum, either self-regulation (thru firms adding environmental accountability to their list of responsibilities

- in addition to authenticity and accessibility, pace Forbes Magazine) or financial disincentives for greenhouse emitting/polluting industries, (TO ENCOURAGE THEM TO TO AVOID THE TAX BY INSTALLING GREENHOUSE POLLUTION ABATEMENT EQUIPMENT)/ providing financial incentives for post industrial / non greenhouse emitting sectors of the economy (meaning providing support for service and primary producing sectors (efforts to revamp towards organic agriculture, reforestation, and restocking the oceans and lakes with fish as well as cleaning up the plastics mess left behind/not to mention cleaning up the Great Lakes, by converting them back to public ownership of common property instead of dumping grounds for private industry/this could also be attempted through appropriate regulation of common property uses/abuses by private firms but good luck with that??!!!)

Too ambitious? Perhaps, perhaps not. Every little bit in the direction of both Plan (a) but especially Plan B would clearly be helpful and move us in the right direction of meeting those crucial reductions in greenhouse emmissions by the target date of 2030, or thereabouts (sooner?).

It is my hope that this book will stimulate others to think and come up with real solutions to the climate change crisis facing our planet today, so that tomorrow will come a better day.

Chris Nelson).

Post Script 2: The Still Great Virtue
of the Modern Capitalist Economy

Much was said in a previous book of mine (Pollyanna's Hope), about the non applicability of the small scale competitive sector in 21st Century Competitive Capitalism. For example John Galbraith portrayed modern capitalism as consisting of a dualism of residual small scale competitive enterprises and a rising sector of large scale long run profit maximizing firms relying on lucrative contracts with the government. Clearly Galbraith left a great deal out in painting such a simple picture of what in reality is a highly complex economy composed of many types of industry and many types of market structure. All this was acknowledged in my previous book. There it was said that the optimal market structure was a mix between competition and oligopoly, following on what my Industrial Organization professor adumbrated to us students way back when. But to say that the 21st Century North American Economy consists in its entirety of such a mix between competition and oligopoly, and to hold this up as the model for all sectors of the economy to follow is also to leave out the greater part of what we know and experience every day on trips for shopping. The great virtue of the old style mom and pop shops small scale competitive sector, sector praised by Adam Smith in his Wealth of Nations was that competition between firms producing a roughly similar product beat down prices and profits to the lowest level consistent with covering costs including the interest opportunity cost of capital) in this manner serving the public interest by providing the consumer with that which he wanted at the price that he wanted - i.e. the lowest price possible. Is he gouged for all he is worth by huge monopolists who restrict output and raise prices in the manner in which Smith most feared? Answer: not at all??!!! There has come into being over the course of the last century a form of business enterprise known as the SALES MAXIMIZING INDUSTRIAL ENTERPRISE. These are large scale retail vendors/sellers that on account of their large size and market power could, if they wanted to/or felt it in their best interests to, easily control their markets by restricting output and raising prices to reap monopoly profits - but do they, in fact, do this? Not at all. Instead, they focus on maximizing sales subject to a "minimum profit constraint" to keep their shareholders content/from griping. How does maximizing sales revenue benefit the large scale enterprise? Well, first of all, it reaps great cost savings from scale economies in sourcing, stocking, and marketing of goods and services. Second, by maximizing sales revenue the enterprise can expand and grow larger over time, rather than just stay the same size were it to restrict output and raise prices in the fashion of a Smithian monopolist. Let us now consider the implications of all this for the consumer. Guess what? We have got in the sales maximizing retailer of today a replacement in terms of the low prices and variety that the consumer wants. And moreover, by emphasizing low cost and low prices, rather than high cost high priced luxuries, the sales maximizer is doing his bit to help the average ordinary person get a larger slice of the economic pie in relation to high income consumers, which would not be the case if the sales maximizer catered to the luxury market instead of the mass market. So there u have it: they produce what the average consumer wants at the lowest possible price which is said to be the great virtue of the modern capitalist economy still.

Chris Nelson).

P.S. Note that the sales maximizing retail vendor, being part of the service sector also fits in nicely with our notions and ideas of the post industrial society, insofar as the products sold are from the consumer goods industry and not heavy machine producing industry, and thus not, so far as I am aware, associated with large

Post Script 3 The "Vital Link" Provided by Small Service Businessman Tending to Local Communities Today

(for to keep job for Chris)

Here mention: plumbers/electricians/home heating/and air conditioning/ lawn cutting/local branches of banks/hedge trimming/underground irrigation experts/barbers/hairdressers/pizzaparlours/cafes/pubs/convenience stores/ scale greenhouse emission/pollution - clothing/footwear/mattresses/ organically grown foodstuffs/hardware/sporting goods/photography/rack/ television phonne/stationary/confectionary/period cars and so on - onwards and upwards.

Steve Forbes in May issue of Forbes magazine said:" all of the above mentioned people are working to make our lives better and easier". Since small businesses are largely competitive (price at lowest cost) and not damaging to the environment, these types of businesses rightly argue that they should not be encumbered/burdened by costly red tape regulations. The need for regulation is seemingly not relevant in the case of these types of small business. Steve Forbes is right.

Monitor service - providers to communities: plumbers/ electrician/ home helpers and air conditioning/ landscapers/ snow removal/ lawn cutlery/ ???/

recycling/ mail men/ public transit/ telephone service and repair/ cable tv service/ internet service/ local banking service ???/ house painters/ roof layers/ hedge ???/ tree planters/ underground irrigation ??? installer/ local doctors/ dentists/ firemen/ policeman/ barbers/ beer/ wine/ food retailers/ hairdressers/ pizza parlors/ ???/ convenience stores/ health food stores/ cáfe / ???

<u>Farber, Steve</u>: ??? in May ??? - all these above mentioned people are working to make our life better and easier when we grow older. - And they should definitely not be encountered by red tape regulation since competition shall ensure fair prices for their services. The need for resolution does not enter her because they are not ??? ecology/ ??? like or a rich to the consumer rather is a only light ??? to big business, using techniques of <u>non production</u>, sometimes involving pollution ??? that the ??? comes into play at all.

Footnote on the Question of the Rate of Torches of Corporations
- whether "Economically Constrained" (Conservation ???) or "Politically Motivated" (liberal ???)

Conservatives argue in favour of local possible ??? or ??? on all types of business (from the military corporation all the way due to your corner grocery store) on the ground that ??? are okay, and everywhere directly related to a healthy climate for investment, growth, and job creation. Let us now examine this down. By putting more money in the hands of the discretion of the business on how to make use of the enterprise's range of choice is increased. It may choose to return the money internally/pay them out or dividend to shareholders / or invest them in expansion of the business, thereby creating new job, and someones growth ??? whether it actually/or potentially/ ??? than last option will depend on whether the business has or has not a suitable market with lucrative opportunities for profitable new ???

In order to be able to invest and create jobs, a necessary condition is that the firm has available internal money & honor the investment; the opportunity to borrow the money at reasonable rules of interest, or be able to offer a new share ???. Only the hard method requires that the firm has cash on hand from referred earners, the other do not.

This does not mean that the trickle down theory, necessarily involved but it does ??? that it's validity will depend on how budget contained the firm in, be how hard it is for the firm to obtain external ??? and/or share ??? money. Personally the business that is short of funds, is not a profitable, and then has greater difficulty in financing externally, shall be the firm that receives the greatest most or this relief at the arm is to keep the firm viable and ??? it growth. This again suggests that for relief should be targeted according to these outers rather than to providing covers the spectrum to relief.

To the extent that the for system dues then the trickle down theory will be validated/ to the extent that it does not, the liberal position that cover the board for relief in politically motivated may be possibly be recorded or being partly politically motivated by a big in form of business interests, that is not profitable in terms of purely economic condition. ???

ECONOMIC THINKERS IN MODERN PERSPECTIVE

THE A B C'S OF LITERACY IN ECONOMIC IDEAS

FOR THE INTELLIGENT LAY PERSON

Post Script 4: The Role of Tax Relief/Tax Breaks to Businesses - Whether Economically Necessary (Conservative Position) or Politically Motivated (Liberal Position)

The proper question to ask: does the business NEED government money to its finance investment and job creation plans. Note that we are assuming that the business has such plans which is predicated on the existence of the needed markets for its product(s) and thus opportunities for profitable investment. However there may be other ways the business can finance the investment rather than lobbying for scarce government financial resources: reinvestment of retained earnings/borrowing the funds at interest from financial institutions and venture capital banks/and last but not lease trading ownership in the public company for funds raised by issuing new share capital.

The validity of the "trickle down theory" (tax breaks being needed to generate new investment and create jobs) depends on how budget constrained firms are/how onerous on the firm are other methods of financing/and whether there the market prospects for their product(s) are sufficiently promising to justify new investment and job creation in the first place.

One conclusion which flows from this brief discussion is that tax relief should, in my humble opinion, be targeted at those firms that actually NEED the money for well thought out and planned investment and job creation programs that they can't finance on their own, creating a case for government assistance for tax relief. There ought also to be follow up to ensure that the relief provided is in fact put to good use financing investment and job creation/not that the firm just sits on the money/like an unconditional present/gift from the government with nothing expected from the firm.

To the extent that the tax relief is targeted to firms who really need it and can make use of it/the trickle down theory will be validated/to the extent that it is not/ as may be the case if it is handed out across the whole spectrum of businesses irrespective of need/ and proven ability to put to good use, the liberal position that trickle down relief is politically motivated gains in credibility as against the argument that it is economically necessary.

Keynes

Secular stagnation is defined as a situation where the rate of economic growth exhibits a long run downward trend over time. Keynes argued the a richer society will save a higher proportion of its GDP than a poorer one on account people gradually becoming satiated with material possessions and thus choosing to consume less and save more. Savings being a withdrawal from the circular flow of income in an economy, this would have a depressing effect on overall demand in an economy. With markets for goods contracting what incentive is there for firms to invest in new capacity and create more jobs? Clearly this presents a serious problem for maintaining a steady rate of growth and job creation via the usual means. Keynes proposed solution was to shift from producing ever more goods which could not find markets/be sold to making a trade involving giving everyone more leisure time which they could use to enjoy the material possessions they already had in abundance (thinking here especially of the upper middle income and upper income classes). So far so good, Keynes' theory makes perfect logical sense/ I am not privy to the extent it is borne out by the empirical evidence. I have heard that one main reason why increased leisure for all has so far not come about is that firms are too greedy for profits. But is not less growth exactly what we need as a society in order to not overburden the planet's already stretched to breaking point carrying capacity?

Some economists have developed an extension of Keynes's secular stagnation theory, by postulating that as societies grow richer, income inequality will often go on the up and up. With a larger proportion of their incomes being saved by high income earners, and with increasing inequality putting a larger share of GDP into the pockets of these same high income earners, it follows that such societies will exhibit higher savings ratios than more equal societies. If people, meaning the upper echelons were to be given more leisure for less income, while the lower echelons were to be given more income for less leisure, two problems might be solved simultaneously. Income inequality would be mitigated at the same time as concentrating leisure on those who can afford it the most, would be good for the environment and respecting the limits to growth so as to remain within/not exceeding the carrying capacity of the planet, habitat for all living creatures, including man (homo sapiens).

Schum

Adam Smith

Adam Smith
was the first bona fide economist.

How markets work, he explained.
That's how he made his name.

He said producing firms free should be profits to seek/by providing goods and services which consumers want and please.

He explained that market forces are like an "Invisible Hand", ensuring a balance between supply (of both goods and labour) and demand.

He showed that competition between rival firms in profits "fair" would result, but under monopoly, might catapult.

He said governments in markets must never intervene for that would wreck and ruin his whole "perfect scheme".

He advocated a policy of laissez-faire, or leave markets alone, he said markets always work best on their own.

His major point was that self interest on the part of profit seeking firms, competing in markets, to the public interest would redound, by giving the consuming public what they want in the round.

He claimed to show all nations of the world the road from poverty to wealth, so many an economist has raised a glass to his very good health. (or at least his ideas)!

Assessment

The first point to note is that the model assumes a world/universe of only small scale competitive firms, examples he chose being the butcher, the baker, the green grocer, and the brewer. (your typical mom and pop shops that still exist today). However, even in his day, (18th century England) this was to ignore the large iron and coal concerns, the textile, the real estate, railway, shipping, and mercantile trading companies. To lump all these disparate firms under one umbrella (small scale competitive markets) is clearly an over-simplification at best, at worst, it may have been a rationalization for non payment of their fair share of taxes by the big companies and or regulation of any harmful activities (e.g. pollution/plunder of nature/consumer protection and protection of the worker). Lastly, Smith's approach rules out any and all role for a public sector and democratically well run government in all but a very few extremely narrow areas of economic endeavour. In other words he gave government a bad name. Who benefits from that? Who benefits most from government programs?

2. Thomas Malthus

Thomas Malthus was anything but an optimist like his Adam Smith peer. He thought prospects for human progress were very dim, on account of his population fears.

The supply of arable land being fixed, he said, meant that, as a species, we were DEAD!

Condemned through food shortages to live perpepetually in dire poverty and need, any increase in real wages would only result in MORE MOUTHS TO FEED!

Wages would thus always be at the level of subsistence bare, population pressure (or employers!) serving to keep them there.

As a prognosticator of human progress in the rich lands he was not (until recently!) much borne out, but his ideas linger on as regards to the poor ones, without any doubt!

The enormous human costs of the population explosion are a gloomy reminder, that we live in a world where resources are FINITE!

Assessment-

For nearly two and a half centuries (2020 is the 250th anniversary of the Industrial Revolution in its English birthplace from whence it spread over the surface of the entire planet, in what is sometimes termed as the European "take-over bid") the system coasted along blithely ignoring the impact of industrial economic activity on mother nature. In fact the whole idea of the industrial revolution was to bend mother nature to man's will so as to create material wealth for man. In the opening decades of the 21st century, man is suddenly realizing that the bounty of mother nature has been taken for granted by him with nary a second or even third thought. Not wishing to litany (refer to the book, Enough is Enough (John Taylor) also my own two books, Pollyanna's Hope and Adaptations), let's just say: man's reckless extravagance in the past has led to nature now presenting the bill to man. Whether man will have the will and the financial and technological capacity to pay up what nature is demanding in the way of a massive cleanup, remains to be seen. (see Adaptations for an alternative less costly approach relying on accellerating the trend towards the service sector and the Post Industrial Society, in cases where industry is unable/unwilling to convert to cleanliness/hygienic methods.)

3. David Ricardo

Ricard, Dave,
was the 1840's apostle of English free trade.

He argued that under the existing high tariffs on imported grain landlords
alone from economic progress would gain.

It was of these same tariffs on imported corn, that their high and rising rents
were born.

Industrial growth placed rising demands on a fixed supply of land, when food
prices rose relatively, workers' subsistence food requirements higher industrial
real wages would command.

These higher real wages into industrial profits would eat, unless these "Corn
Laws" were soon repealed.

This soon became the "hottest issue" of the day, the balance of political power
was shifting the industrialists' way.

And it was this reality which the government finally did sway, to abolish the
duties on imported grain!

Assessment

Some would argue that what the government "should" have done was to keep the duties but abolish landlordism (land to the tiller). The tillers of the soil and workers in industry would have reaped more of the benefits of industrial growth that way.

What relevance has Ricardo to the modern world. Many developing countries are importers of foodstuffs and face a choice of either catering to the farm population or catering to the desire of industry for low real wage supply of labour. Some limited protection for agriculture preserves this sector in larger size and scale than if everyone ends up being crammed into factories at low wages. As such, agriculture is often referred to by progressive economists as the "handmaiden of growth".

4. Wilfredo Pereto

Pereto was a very smart guy, a sort of 19th century economic genie,. He developed a three-part concept of economic/allocative efficiency.

At the highest level of generalization, "efficiency" is defined as a situation where it is impossible to improve the "material happiness" of even one person in society without reducing that of another commensurately.

The "economic happiness" of society is thus "maximized" - for any given distribution of income - when this condition is fully satisfied.

Efficiency in production, consumption, and product-mix is said to be best achieved under a "laissez-faire", "lassez passez', capitalist market economy. (a simple set of three mathematical conditions is satisfied at the margin).

Society's scarce resources of capital and labour are used to best effect, when all three of these conditions are fully met!

For any desired distribution of the "economic pie", these three conditions guarantee its maximum size!

The Paretian model leaves out of consideration, besides capital and labour, environmental and energy inputs, to productive processes. It is common knowledge that today one is becoming more concerned with "environmental efficiency", and the "quality of life" over and above the mere "quantity of material possessions" which critics often term "GNP'ism" or excessive concern with eternal/everlasting growth of GNP. Nevertheless it is good to know the meaning of efficiency in this traditional sense of the word as well, especially in society's at a low level of development where the name of the game is still to make best use of scarce resources to raise material standards of living.

5. Arthur Pigou

The water we drink, the air we breathe, and certain types of land uses that are free, are three resources which are "common property."

No single individual or firm these resources does own. Thus, there is no incentive to look after and protect them as is well known!

The result of this lack of protection is a "global gardyloo"* where common property becomes a "dumping ground" for wastes, be they industrial or human, too!

In terms of welfare economics (Pigou), this is said to respresent a DIVERGENCY between PRIVATE COSTS of production, and costs borne by the WHOLE OF SOCIETY!

In theory, the CORRECTION OF SUCH DIVERGENCIES requires a TAX ON THE DIFFERENCE, thus making firms (hopefully!) CUT BACK ON PODUCTION or, IF POSSIBLE, INSTALL POLLUTION ABATEMENT EQUIPMENT!

BUT IN PRACTICE, SOCIAL COSTS OFTEN CANNOT BE MEASURED IN TERMS CUT AND DRIED (I.E. IN TERMS OF DOLLARS AND CENTS) FOR THE NECESSARY CORRECTIVE TAXES TO BE APPLIED.

---

*	gardyloo: in medieval times when washer women prepared to throw slops into the street below from balconies above they would warn people to get out of the way by crying "garde de l'eau" or beware the water.

SO THAT THE REMEDY FOR THIS "SAD STATE OF AFFAIRS"/
REQUIRES "VALUE JUDGMENTS" AND GOVERNMENT
REGULATION AND RULES OF THOSE WHO WOULD POLLUTE
OUR PRECIOUS LAND/WATER/AND AIR!!!!!

——

Assessment-

Canadian water, in our lakes and rivers used to be publicly owned and
protected against polluters/with the coming of the North American Free
Trade Agreement, in 1989, water fell into private hands who ofen used it as
a dumping grounds.

6. Marx, Karl

Marx, Karl,'
at capitalism did SNARL!

He thought that under capitalism "man exploited man". That all this talk of
"common interests" between workers and management, was just a sham.

He thought that capitalism would eventually croak, on account of too many
"unemployed folk".

AUTOMATION would blue collar workers out of work throw. Eventually
workers and capitalists would come to blows.

When his foresight proved faulty concerned especially the Rise of the Educated
Middle Classes, his much too simple model applied, if at all, only to the
industrial systems of the distant past!

He thought that the answer was to make ALL Capital Publicly Owned and
Operated, so that capitalist could no longer grind workers to the bone/and
automation would never be introduced without worker consent/cooperation!
(Again: lack of foresight - public enterprises, being budget based have NO
incentive to cut costs and be efficient in their use of resources so they often end
up becoming sinecure havens for over-supplied PhD graduates sitting around
doing precious little according to friend of mine)

A number of facts put the lie to Marx's main arguments criticisms/ NAMELY:

growth of corporate responsibility to workers and the community government demand management (a la Kaynes /see next entry) as a means of beating back the business cycle/ and the growth in many lands of social spending/

To put it in the simplest possible terms; CAPITALISM ALWAYS FOUND A WAY ITS FLAWS OF MENDING...!!!!!!

AND SOCIALISM OF THE SOVIET COMMUNIST KIND COMPLETELY FAILED HIS HOPES TO FULFILL; NOT ONLY WAS THAT REVOLUTION CORRUPTED BY THE EMERGENCE OF A TOTALITARIAN DICTATORSHIP/BUT THERE WAS ALWAYS A DEARTH OF CONSUMER GOODS AND LONG LINE-UPS OUTSIDE SHABBY FOOD DISTRIBUTION SHOPS, WHILE "RICH COUNTRY CAPITALISM NEVER HAD ANY PROBLEM GIVING MOST PEOPLE "THE GOOD LIFE" OR IN FEEDING ITS POP'S.

Assessment -

Self Explanatory- Communism collapsed/Capitalism Bravely Marches onwards and upwards...

7. John Maynard Keynes

Everybody knows that John Maynard Keynes, was an INCREDIBLE BRAIN.

In the DIRTY THIRTIES he wrote his book called "The General Theory" for workers and families who had of MASS UNEMPLOYMENT grown weary!

The problem of the jobless can be very tricky. When wages are too high and "DOWNWARD STICKY" i.e. not prone to be flexible and fall/rise with the ebb and flow of business activity.

The problem of the Unemployed is especially tough, when consumers and businesses out of their "empty pockets" AREN'T SPENDING ENOUGH!

BUT IF (AND THAT CANNOT BE TAKEN ALWAYS FOR GRANTED IF GOVERNMENTS HAVE ACCUMULATED A HIGH DEBT BURDEN AND DEBT SERVICE BURDEN FROM PAST PROFLIGACY)

BUT AGAIN! IF GOVERNMENTS HAVE MONEY TO SPARE, AGGREGATE DEMAND- OR TOTAL DEMAND FOR ALL GOODS AND SERVICES THAT A GIVEN ECONOMY PRODUCES ON YEARLY BASIS

AGGREGATE DEMAND THEY CAN BOOST, ARGUED KEYNES, BY PUTTING IT THERE - IN THOSE "EMPTY POCKETS"!

WITH MULTIPLIER EFFECTS MAGNIFYING THE INITIAL SHOT IN THE ECONOMY'S ARM THROUGH MULTIPLE ROUNDS

OF SPENDING/GDP WILL GO ON THE UP AND UP THUS THE PROBLEM OF DEFICIENT DEMAND A' MENDING!

WITH "CONFIDENCE" IN THE ECONOMY BEING RESTORED BUSINESS WILL INVEST AND CONSUMERS WILL START SPENDING MORE!

WHEN FIRMS BEGIN HIRING AGAIN, THAT'S A SURE SIGN THAT THE ECONOMY IS ON THE MEND!

WHEN EQUILIBRIUM (STABLE POSITION) HAS BEEN REACHED AT THE LEVEL OF "EMPLOYMENT FULL" that's the PROOF THAT THE GOVERNMENT THE ECONOMY OUT OF RECESSION DID PULL!

Assessment -

While Keynes' idea is basically sound, it has sometimes been used as a kind of "trojan horse", or excuse, to sneak in spendthrift policies which drain the public purse of funds needed when the next recession comes along but the government of the day, on account the cupboards being and/or bare, has no money to spare for combatting recession. Thus for Keyne's methods to work governments must impose financial discipline on themselves and those in their employ.

A Brief Word on Keynes's Theory Concerning the Possibility of "Secular Stagnation"

Secular stagnation is defined as a situation where the role of economic growth show a love ??? at award decline eventually resulting in a state of gene growth. - The claimed economic called this the "stationary state" and viewed it as a normal outcome of "diminishing ???". The reclaimed economic introduced the concept of "technological program" and "the growth of the ??? capital" or educational manpower as a mean to that this claimed conclusion Keynes added a further ??? to the strong by introduction the possibility that a society grow higher a steadly increase ??? would be saved which would ??? in the ??? side."

Is a twist, further some economity postulate growing inequality of income distribution. With a longer program of income being covered by high income earner ??? the rest of the population, the tendency for the ??? to rise would further be ??? one further ???

8. Milton Friedmann

Why the 1970's Reality from the traditional "trade off" theory did swerve, Friedman explained with his expectations - augmented Phillips Curve.

In the short run when the overall price level does rise (inflation), real wages become cheaper so firms more workers do hire.

But when workers next at the bargaining table are sitting, they will surely ask for higher wages to protect their standard of living.

Thus real wages become dearer again, so firms will hire fewer working men.

In this way, Friedmann explained the paradox of rising prices, together at one and the same time with rising joblessness, which had completely baffled traditional trade-off theorists.

With his concept of "inflationary expectations "he built on the old classical idea that workers are "rational" and bargain for wages "real"!

The theory of the tradeoff had assumed "money illusion" which Friedman correctly pointed out implied not rationality, but "self-delusion"!

Assessment -

with Friedmann came a shift from "fighting unemployment" using fiscal policy to "fighting inflation" using monetary policy as his tool. Friedmann, a follower of Adam Smith, was anti government dogmatic/ and dogmatically in favour of laissez faire / laissez passer / economics. His ideas were very influential in government and business circles, less so among the left leaning media and writers of books.

9. Harold Innis

Harold Innis's "staples theory of economic growth," that's the uniquely "CANADIAN" contribution to "economic folklore".

The regions of Canada each specialized in specific "staple resources" at one time in their history/that fitted the bill of "EXCHANGE GOOD" to the English MOTHER COUNTRY.

The COD of the Grandbanks, the FUR of the Beaver, and FOREST LUMBER, were followed by GOLD, MINERALS, and PRAIRE WHEAT, all at one time played the role' of regional STAPLE COMMODITY.

The STAPLE GOOD the LEADING SECTOR of each REGIONAL ECONOMY did comprise, "HEALTHY DEVELOPMENT OCCURS WHEN AROUND THESE RAW GOODS THE ECONOMY SUCCESSFULLY DIVERSIFIES!

Producing the inputs, processing the output, as well as producing consumer goods for the home market so created is the aim, ADDING VALUE is THE NAME OF THE GAME, the potential for successful diversification around the EXPORT BASE" depends on the STAPLE TECHNOLOGY/REGION INTERFACE.

Innis called them backward, forward, and final demand "linkages" respectively, the larger they are the more the region and it's people's benefit prospectively.

The relevance of his ideas has never been greater. not only to the regions Canadian, but also to small Third World "staple exporting nations"!

Assessment -

remains a valuable way of understanding the economics of regional specializations both within individual lands/ and within all geographically differentiated space.

10. Joseph Schumpeter

TECHNOLOGY TO THE RESCUE, was Schumpeter's theme. THOUGH JUST HOW (?) remains to be seen.

THE CAUSE OF LONG RUN RECESSION is DEMAND SATIATION there is ONLY ONE SOLUTION: NEW PRODUCT INNOVATION! (or, MORE LEISURE FOR ALL as in Keynes' more humanitarian prognostication).**

New product technology CREATES FOR NEW INVESTMENT THE POTENTIAL: AS OLD PRODUCTS ARE DISPLACED AND NEW ONES MARKETS DO ENTER!

"CREATIVE DESTRUCTION" WAS THE NAME HE COINED FOR THIS, FOR WITH NEW PRODUCTS, WHOLE NEW INDUSTRIES DO EMERGE AND FLOURISH!

---

*   Under Keynes's ??? for all prognostication GDP would remain stable/constant at full employment level of GDP. With continuing advances in science and technology, productivity of ??? will keep on gang up and up over time, the DIFFERENCE being that wherein formerly productivity increases led to more goods and services being produced; now productivity increases enable workers to have increasing marks of leisure time to do with as they please. All this is exactly in keeping with the ecological requirement of the plant i.e. that the limits to growth be respected.

IF "NECESSITY IS THE MOTHER OF INVENTION," then ENCOURAGING RESEARCH AND DEVELOPMENT (R&D) MAY BE THE ANSWER TO LONG RUN RECESSION!

Schumpeter a WORD OF WARNING to capitalism did issue, exaggerated a trifle, he predicted that growing firm size and BUREAUCRATIZATION NEW INNOVATION WOULD STIFLE!

GOVERNMENTS IN PRIVATE ECONOMIC AFFAIRS MIGHT ACTIVELY ENGAGE, PUBLIC SPENDING AND TAXATION WOULD OUT OF HAND GROW, WITH THE DEMISE OF LAISSEZ FAIRE/LAISSEZ PASSER APPROACH/CAPITALISM MIGHT EVEN...... FAIL!

BUT HAPPILY, HE WAS MOSTLY WRONG WITH HIS GLOOMY PROGNOSTICATION/FOR DESPITE GROWING FIRM SIZE AND GOVERNMENT INTERVENTIONISM/CAPITALISM CONTINUES TO LEAD/REMAINS AT THE PINNACLE OF NEW PRODUCT INNOVATION!

Assessment -

The question of moment is: if society has "enough" of material goods - i.e. is SATIATED - why not LIMIT GROWTH and give people MORE TIME OFF, THAT IS TO SAY, LONGER UNPAID VACATIONS so that with given wage bill/budget for employment, a firm will be able to employ more workers. Along with a trend towards growing leisure time was expected another trend in modern capitalism - NAMELY THE TREND AWAY FROM THE MANUFACTURING SECTOR ON ACCOUNT OF AUTOMATION DISPLACING BLUE COLLAR WORKERS THERE AT THE SAME TIME AS GROWING AFFLUENCE IS SHIFTING DEMAND IN FAVOUR OF THE LEISURE LIFE STYLE CATERING SERVICE SECTOR, HERALDING THE EMERGENCE OF THE POST INDUSTRIAL SOCIETY OF THE FUTURE. (AS NOTED ELSEWHERE/ IF INDUSTRY IS THE PROBLEM WHEN IT COMES TO CLIMATE CHANGE AND THE ECOLOGICAL CRISIS IN GENERAL____

THEN MIGHT NOT THE ACCELERATING OF EXISTING TRENDS TOWARDS NON POLLUTING SERVICE SECTOR OF THE POST INDUSTRIAL SOCIETY TO COME_____ be THE EASIEST AND LEAST COSTLY ANSWER??!!!

About the Author

A cat named birdie/adaptations too - Christopher Richard nelson was born on December 24, 1956 in the town of Baden-Baden, West Germany (black forest). the only son of his English father, Thomas Donald, and his German wife, Rosemarie, he lived in Canada (Ontario and Quebec), Europe (Fontainebleau, France) and the States (Colorado Springs, Colorado). A Master's Scholar in Economic Science, Chris has worked for the federal government (NRC/Finance) before circumstances led him to take up free lance writing: ten first class/original books with emphasis on global challenges (Holistic Economic Development) and Christian vs. Worldly Value Systems and their implications for humanity's happiness/survival (depending on peace, social justice, and stewardship of mother nature's resources/habitats for plants and animals including man) (Pollyanna's Hope and Adaptations). Chris also likes to write light hearted/amusing poetry about the people and pets in his life: A Single Rose Can be My Garden (with four subtitles) and A Cat Named Birdie (also including A Budgie Named Bertie).